AF587513

PEGASUS ENCYCLOPEDIA LIBRARY

# Physics

# WAVES AND SOUND

Edited by: Anil Kumar Tomar, Pallabi B. Tomar
Managing editor: Tapasi De
Designed by: Vijesh Chahal, Anil Kumar and Rohit Kumar
Illustrated by: Suman S. Roy, Tanoy Choudhury
Colouring done by: Vinay Kumar, Sonu, Kiran Kumari & Pradeep Kumar

# CONTENTS

# Waves: An introduction

The term 'wave' has many meanings in everyday language. When we hear the word 'wave', the first picture that comes in mind is of ocean waves or a friend waving his hand to us. We may not necessarily think of sound or light, but we should know that they are also a kind of waves. However, the previous examples are useful in understanding waves. They tell us that a wave is a periodic disturbance or vibration in a medium. The ocean waves are a disturbance of the water while the waving of hand creates disturbance in the air and the motion in both cases is periodic. To understand waves in better way, first, we need to understand the concepts of vibratory and periodic motions.

The three basic types of motions are translator, rotatory and vibratory motion. **Translator motion** is defined as motion of an object along a straight line or along a given path. The motion which is around a centre point in concentric circles is **rotatory motion**. The motion of an object moving to and fro about a fixed point is **vibratory motion**.

When an object is displaced from its fixed position and made to move to and fro periodically, it is known as vibratory motion. A vibratory motion happens when a particle oscillates to and fro from its position. Thus, it is also called as **oscillatory motion**. Real life application of vibratory motion can be seen in musical instruments especially the string instruments, speakers, in light bulbs and swings.

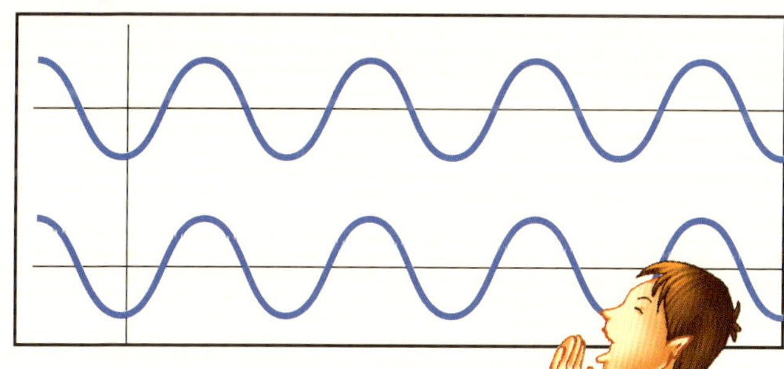

## Do it yourself

**Sound box:** Collect a shoe box and elastic bands. Put the elastics around the box. Use your finger to pluck each elastic. Listen to the different sounds. Use the fingers of one hand to stretch one of the elastics. Pluck the elastic. Does it change the note?

The elastics vibrate when they are plucked. Both the vibrating object and the tension will change the sound. Wide elastics usually vibrate slower, so they create low notes. Thin elastics vibrate faster to create higher notes. A loose elastic will vibrate more slowly (creating a lower note) than a tight elastic that is the same width.

There are two types of vibratory motions—free vibratory motion and forced vibratory motion. When we only apply initial force to make an object vibrate and then allow it to vibrate freely, a free vibration occurs. The frequency of these motions reduces gradually and finally come to a zero when the swing comes to a halt. This is called a free vibratory motion. Forced vibration is when a force is applied to an object at regular intervals to cause a regular to and fro motion in the object. In forced vibration the frequency of the to and fro motion of the object along a fixed point does not reduce gradually, instead the frequency is dependent upon the force applied.

## Simple pendulum: an example of vibratory motion

A simple pendulum is a classic example of vibratory motion. A simple pendulum consists of a point mass suspended by a cord of negligible mass at a fixed point. The length of the pendulum is the distance from the point of suspension to the centre of gravity. The resting position of a simple pendulum is known as the mean position.

When the pendulum is displaced to an angle and released, the pendulum swings to and fro with periodic motion against the fixed point. This motion is called a vibratory motion. One complete to and fro movement of a pendulum about its mean position is known as an oscillation or vibration. During an oscillation, the maximum displacement from its mean position is called amplitude. The time taken for one oscillation is known as the time period. The number of oscillations made by the pendulum in one second is called its frequency.

Laws of a simple pendulum

1. The period is independent of its mass, size, shape or material.
2. The period is independent of the amplitude of oscillation.
3. The period is directly proportional to the square root of length of the pendulum.
4. The period is inversely proportional to the square root of the acceleration due to gravity.

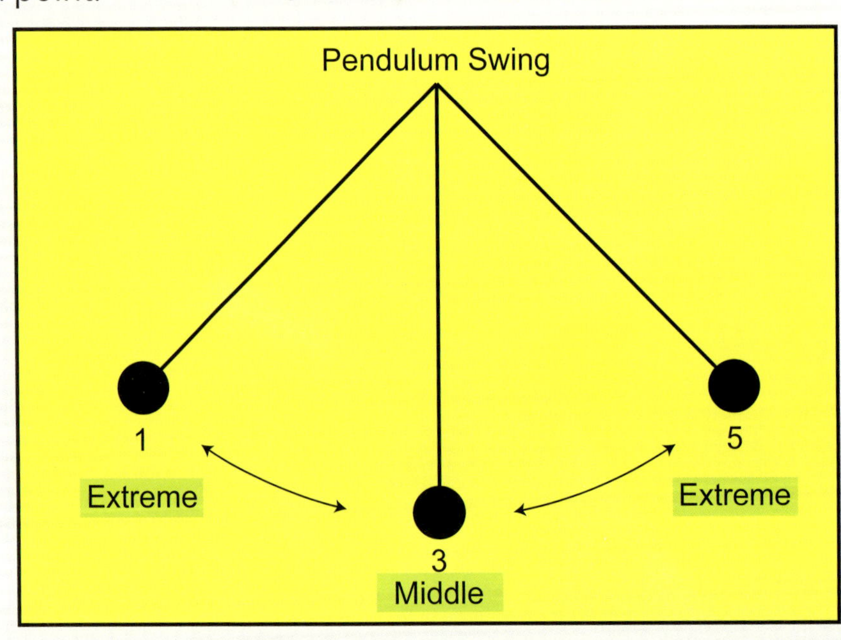

## Periodic motion

The motion of a clock's hands, the motion of the blades of a fan and motion of a planet around the sun continuously repeat their paths. They are examples of repetitive motion. Any point in the path of the body is crossed by the body in the same direction at regular intervals. While, the motion of a body attached to a suspended spring, the motion of the prongs of an excited tuning fork, the motion of the pendulum, the motion of the balance wheel of a watch are also examples of periodic motion but their motion is oscillatory such that they oscillate to and fro about a fixed point. A given point in the path is crossed by the body at regular intervals but in opposite directions. This is called oscillatory motion. All oscillatory motions are periodic but not all periodic motions are oscillatory.

Let us consider an oscillating system, like a mass loaded on a spring. The most important properties involved in the system are elasticity and inertia. When we apply force to extend the spring, it opposes the change in its shape. Restoring force develops in the spring as soon the deforming force is removed and the spring bounces back to its original shape. This property is called elasticity. While returning to its normal state, it overshoots its position of equilibrium. This happens

because of inertia which tries to keep the spring in a state of motion. The spring which is compressed now, tries to attain the normal state. This process repeats itself and the body attached to the spring oscillates.

Within the elastic limits, the deformation produced in a body is proportional to the restoring force. Thus,

$F \alpha y$

And,

$F = -K. y$

Where, K is the force constant for the spring and negative sign indicates the tendency of the force to restore the body to its equilibrium state. The force constant for the spring is known as spring constant.

The body attached to the spring executes oscillations under the action of a force which is always directed towards the equilibrium position and always proportional to its displacement from that position. The motion is not only periodic, but also bounded i.e., the displacement on either side of the equilibrium position is confined within well-defined limits. These functions are called harmonic functions. The musical instruments also involve motions of this type in their air columns or stretched strings.

The motion in which a body oscillates on either side of its equilibrium position under the action of a force is called simple harmonic motion. This force is proportional to the displacement and always directed towards the equilibrium position, in the absence of all frictional forces. The oscillation of a pendulum is considered simple harmonic if the amplitude is small. It is very clear that acceleration in simple harmonic motion is not a constant and hence, the equations of motion of bodies with uniform acceleration cannot be applied.

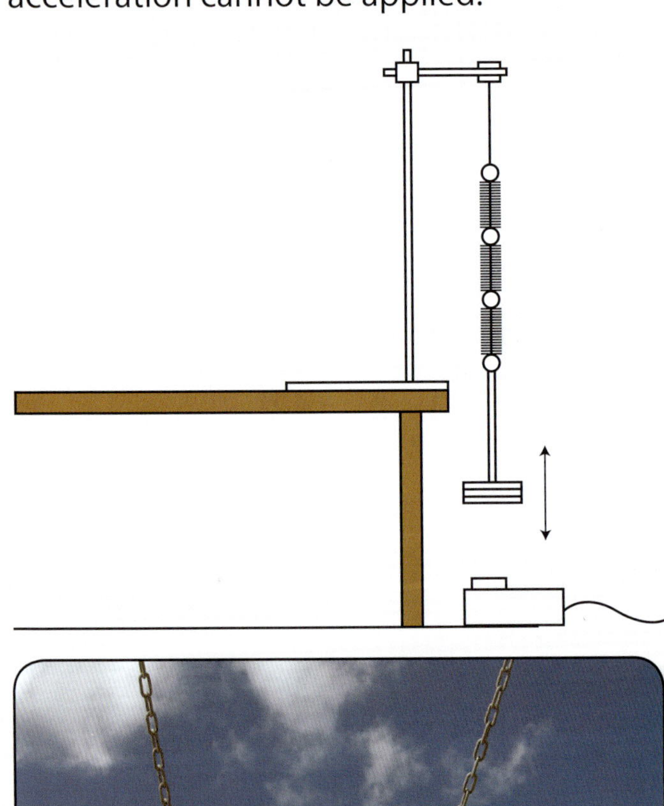

# Waves and wave like motions

Sound waves, visible light waves, radio waves, microwaves, water waves, sine waves, cosine waves, stadium waves, earthquake waves, waves on a string, and slinky waves are just a few examples of the waves. We recognize waves or not, is perhaps not an important thing to ponder but we all encounter waves on a daily basis as they are everywhere. For many of us, the first thought concerning waves makes a picture of a wave moving across the surface of an ocean, lake, pond or any other body of water.

In addition to waves, there are a number of phenomena that resemble waves so closely that we can describe such phenomenon as being wavelike. The motion of a pendulum, the motion of a mass suspended by a spring, and the motion of a child on a swing are commonly considered as wavelike phenomena.

The waves are created by some form of a disturbance, such as a rock thrown into the water. The water wave has a crest and a trough and travels from one location to another. One crest is often followed by a second crest that is often followed by a third crest and so on. Every crest is separated by a trough to create an alternating pattern of crests and troughs.

## Do it yourself

**Seeing sound:** Tie a piece of thread to some tissue paper. Put on some loud music and hold the thread in front of a loud speaker. Watch what happens. Try different types of music and see what happens. Now try changing the volume.

**Explanation:** The sound vibrations make the tissue paper shake.

The waves may appear to be plane waves that travel together as a front in a straight-line direction, perhaps towards a sandy shore. The waves may also be circular waves that originate from the point where the disturbances occur; such circular waves travel across the surface of the water in all directions.

Our understanding of the physical world is not complete until we understand the nature, properties and behaviors of waves. One of the good examples is a football stadium where the crowd is enthusiastically engaged in doing the wave. When performed with reasonably good timing, a noticeable ripple is produced that travels around the stadium back and forth. The observable ripple results when a group of enthusiastic fans rise up from their seats, swing their arms up high, and then sit back down. This can be understood the following way, the viewers in first row abruptly rise up to begin the wave; as they sit back down, row 2 begins its motion and similarly when row 2 sits back down, row 3 begins its motion. This process continues, as each consecutive row becomes involved by a momentary standing up and sitting down. The wave moves from one row to another as each individual member of the row becomes temporarily displaced out seat and returns to it as the wave passes by.

Another good example is rope jumping. All of us have memories of childhood of holding a long jump rope with a friend and vibrating an end up and down. The up and down vibration at one end of the rope creates a disturbance in the rope. This subsequently moves towards the other end of the rope. When it reaches the opposite end, the disturbance bounces back and returns to the end we are holding. A single disturbance can be created by a single vibration at one end of the rope.

The repeated disturbance results in a repeated and regular vibration of the rope. The shape of the wave pattern formed in the rope is influenced by the frequency at which we vibrate it. When we vibrate the rope rapidly, a short wave is created and if we vibrate the rope less frequently, a long wave is created. So, the size of this wave is inversely related to the frequency of the wave created.

We are familiar with radio waves and sound waves. Though we have never seen them, yet we believe they exist. This is because we have witnessed the signals that they carry from one location to another. We have learned to tune into these signals through use of a tuner on a television or radio. Waves carry energy from one location to another.

Thus, a wave is defined as a disturbance that transfers energy progressively from point to another point in a medium. This wave may take the form of an elastic deformation of pressure, electric or magnetic intensity, electric potential, or temperature.

# Classification of waves

The waves can be classified in various ways. One of the ways to categorize waves is on the basis of the direction of movement of the individual particles of the medium relative to the direction that the waves travel. This basis defines waves in two categories, transverse waves, longitudinal waves and surface waves.

## Transverse waves

A transverse wave is defined as a wave in which particles of the medium move in a direction perpendicular to the direction that the wave moves. Thus, the wave moves in one direction and it creates a disturbance in a different direction. Most kinds of waves are transverse waves. The most familiar example of this is the waves on the surface of water. As the wave travels in one direction, it creates an up-and-down motion on the water's surface.

## Longitudinal waves

A longitudinal wave is a wave in which particles of the medium move in a direction parallel to the direction that the wave moves in. These waves can be understood by a medium as a series of particles connected by springs. As one individual particle is disturbed, it transmits the disturbance to the next interconnected particle. This disturbance continues to be passed on to the next particle. The result is that energy is transported from one end of the medium to the other end of the medium without the actual transport of

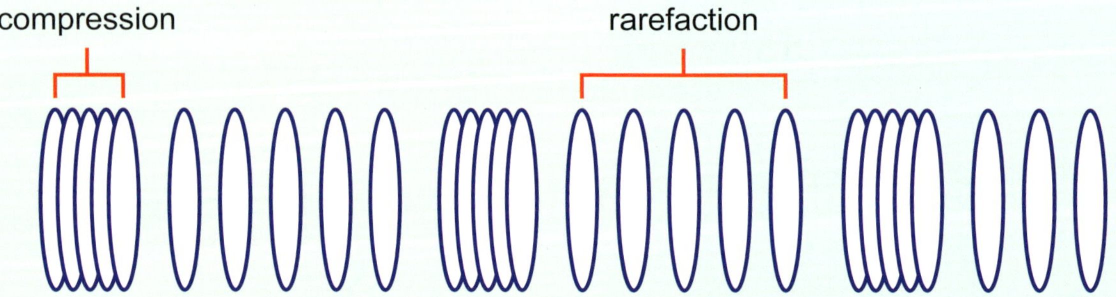


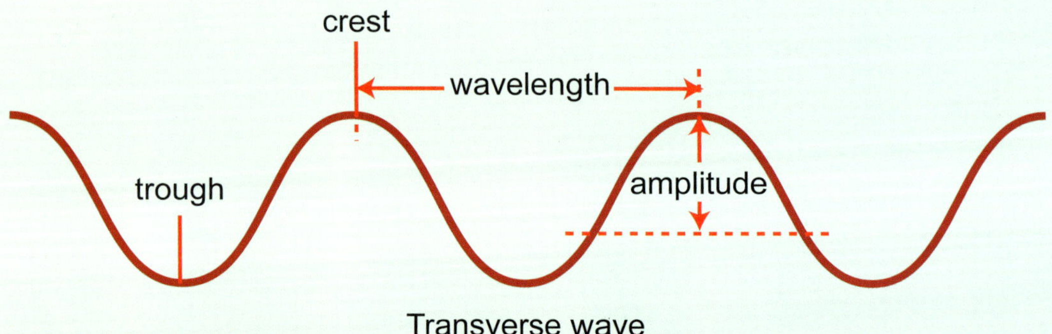

Transverse wave

matter. In this type of wave, the particles of the medium vibrate in a direction parallel to the direction of energy transport.

Waves travelling through a solid medium can either be transverse waves or longitudinal waves while waves travelling through the bulk of a fluid are always longitudinal waves. Transverse waves require a relatively rigid medium in order to transmit their energy. As one particle begins to move it must be able to exert a pull on its nearest neighbour. If the medium is not rigid as is the case with fluids, the particles will slide past each other. Earthquakes are capable of producing both transverse and longitudinal waves that travel through the solid structures of the Earth. Only longitudinal waves are capable of travelling through the core of the Earth. Thus, geologists believe that the Earth's core consists of a liquid.

## Surface waves

A surface wave is a wave in which particles of the medium undergo a circular motion. While waves that travel within the depths of the ocean are longitudinal waves, the waves that travel along the surface of the oceans are referred to as surface waves. In longitudinal and transverse waves, all the particles of the medium move in a parallel or a perpendicular direction relative to the direction of energy transport. But, in a surface wave, it is only the particles at the surface of the medium that undergo the circular motion. The motion of particles tend to decrease as one proceeds further from the surface.

The waves can also be categorized on the basis of their ability or inability to transmit energy through a vacuum. Based on this, waves can be classified as electromagnetic waves and mechanical waves.

## Electromagnetic waves

An electromagnetic wave is a wave that is capable of transmitting its energy through vacuum. These waves are produced by the vibration of charged particles. Electromagnetic waves, produced in the sun, travel to the Earth through the vacuum of outer space. The light waves are examples of electromagnetic waves.

## Mechanical waves

A mechanical wave can be defined as a wave that is not capable of transmitting its energy through vacuum. Thus, these waves require a medium in order to transport their energy from one location to another. A sound wave is a mechanical wave. Sound waves are incapable of travelling through a vacuum. Other examples of mechanical waves are slinky waves, water waves, stadium waves, and jumping rope waves. Each of these waves requires some medium in order to exist. A water wave requires water, a stadium wave requires viewers in a stadium and a jump rope wave requires a jump rope.

# Graphical representation of waves

Whenever a wave passes through a medium, there is a change in some property of the medium. Hence, the waves can be graphically represented by showing the changes in the value of any such property of the medium as the waves travel through it.

## Longitudinal waves

The longitudinal waves travel in the form of compressions and rarefactions and always a compression follows a rarefaction or vice versa. Whenever there is compression, the density of particles of the medium is higher than the normal density, while in a rarefaction, the density of the particles is lower than the normal density. In the distance-density graph for a longitudinal wave, a horizontal straight line represents the normal density of the medium. All the points above this line represent higher densities and the points below this line represent lower densities than the normal density. The particle density at any particular point on a longitudinal wave alternatively increases and decreases with time at regular intervals.

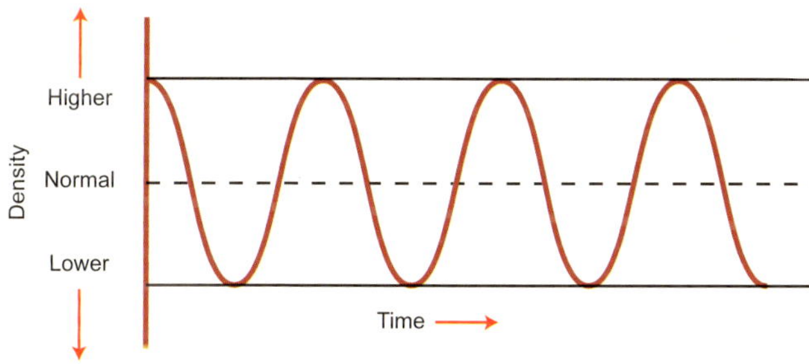


## Transverse waves

Transverse waves propagate in the form of crests and troughs, that is, some particles get displaced upwards, while some others downwards from their mean positions.

A transverse wave dampens after travelling some distance that is, with time.

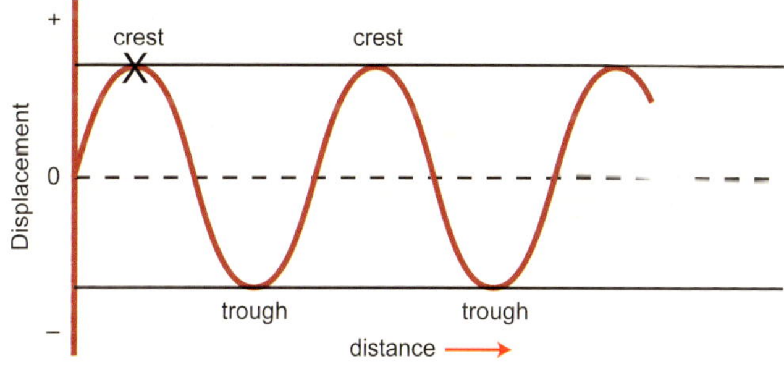


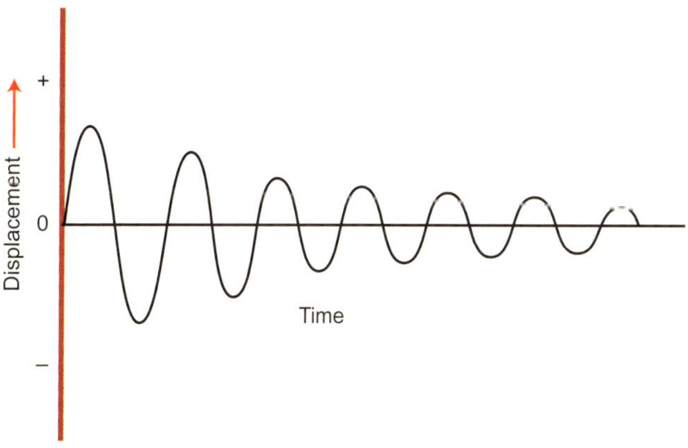

# Wavelength, frequency and period of a wave

We know that wavelength, frequency and time period are the basic elements that describe a wave.

## Wavelength

The wavelength of a wave can be defined as the distance between the two nearest points on the wave. It can also be defined as the distance between two consecutive crests or troughs or the distance between two consecutive compressions or rarefactions.

HIGHER FREQUENCY
shorter wavelength

LOWER FREQUENCY
longer wavelength

Wavelength is denoted by $\lambda$ (pronounced as lambda). Its unit is same as the unit of length such as metre.

## Time period

Time period of a wave is the time taken by a vibrating particle to make one complete vibration. It is defined as the time taken by a wave to move a distance equal to its wavelength. It is denoted by T. Its unit is second.

## Frequency

Frequency is the number of vibrations completed by a particle in one second. It can also be defined as the number of waves passing through a point in one second. The unit of frequency is hertz (Hz).

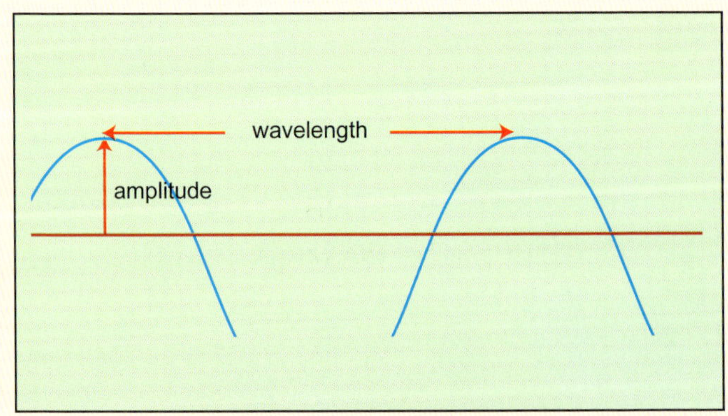

## Relation between frequency and time-period

Let $\nu$ be the frequency of a wave. That means the number of vibrations completed by a particle in one second is $\nu$.

Time taken to complete $\nu$ vibrations = 1 second

Thus, time taken to complete 1 vibration will be equal to $1/\nu$

We know that time taken to complete one vibration is time period of the wave

$$T = 1/\nu$$

Thus,

$$\nu T = 1$$

## Relation between wave-velocity, frequency and wavelength

Wave velocity is defined as the distance traveled by the wave in one second.

Wave velocity = Distance traveled by wave / time

V = wavelength/ time

$= \lambda / T$

We know that,

$$T = 1/\nu$$

Thus, $\nu = 1/T$

$$V = \lambda / \nu$$

Wave velocity = Wavelength  frequency

## Do it yourself

**Violin cup:** Poke a small hole in the bottom of a disposable plastic cup. Cut a piece of string about 1 ft. long and thread it through the hole in the cup. Tie a knot at the end of the string to hold it in place. Wet the string or rub it with a piece of violin rosin. Hold the cup in one hand and pinch the string between the thumb and index finger of your other hand. Slide your fingers down the string, squeezing tightly. The string will make a sound like screeching violins that is caused by vibrations in the string. The rosin or water increases the friction, allowing the string to vibrate more and produce a louder sound. The cup helps amplify the sound.

# Energy transport and the amplitude of a wave

As far we know that a wave is an energy transport phenomenon that transports energy along a medium without transporting matter. The amount of energy carried by a wave is related to the amplitude of the wave. A high energy wave is characterized by high amplitude; a low energy wave is characterized by low amplitude. The amplitude of a wave refers to the maximum amount of displacement of a particle on the medium from its rest position. The amplitude of a transverse pulse is related to the energy which that pulse transports through the medium. Putting a lot of energy into a transverse pulse will not affect the wavelength, the frequency or the speed of the pulse. The energy imparted to a pulse will only affect the amplitude of that pulse.

Different materials have differing degrees of springiness or elasticity. A more elastic medium will tend to offer less resistance to the force and allow a greater amplitude pulse to travel through it; being less rigid (and therefore more elastic), the same force causes greater amplitude. A high energy ocean wave can do considerable damage to the rocks and piers along the shoreline when it crashes upon it.

The energy transported by a wave is directly proportional to the square of the amplitude of the wave. This means that a doubling of the amplitude of a wave is indicative of a fourfold increase of the energy transported by the wave. A tripling of the amplitude of a wave is indicative of a nine-fold increase in the amount of energy transported by the wave and so on.

## Do it yourself

**Strange sound:** Take a 1/4 inch hex nut and squeeze it through the mouth of a large balloon. Carefully blow up the balloon and tie the end of it. Hold the balloon in your palm and move it in a circular motion; the hex nut will begin to make circles inside the balloon and will eventually make a loud noise. The noise is caused when the flat sides of the hex nut come into contact with the balloon, causing vibrations.

# The speed of a wave

A wave is a disturbance that moves along a medium from one end to the other. If one watches an ocean wave moving along the medium, one can observe that the crest of the wave is moving from one location to another over a given interval of time. The crest is observed to cover distance. The speed of an object refers to how fast an object is moving and is usually expressed as the distance traveled per time of travel. In the case of a wave, the speed is the distance travelled by a given point on the wave (such as a crest) in a given interval of time. In equation form,

If the crest of an ocean wave moves a distance of 20 m in 10 seconds, then the speed of the ocean wave is 2 m/s. The faster wave travels a greater distance in the same amount of time. Sometimes a wave encounters the end of a medium and the presence of a different medium.

If a sound wave travels 500 m in 1 second, the speed of the wave is

500 m/s. Reflection phenomena are commonly observed with sound waves. The sound wave travels through the medium, reflects off another medium and returns to its origin. The result is that we hear the echo (that is, the reflected sound wave) of our sound.

## The Wave equation

The wave equation states the mathematical relationship between the speed, wavelength and frequency of a wave.

# Interference of waves

When two or more waves simultaneously and independently travel through the same medium at the same time, their effects are super positioned. The result of that superposition is called interference. There are two types of interference—constructive and destructive.

1. **Constructive interference** occurs when the wave amplitudes reinforce each other, building a wave of even greater amplitude.
2. **Destructive interference** occurs when the wave amplitudes oppose each other, resulting in waves of reduced amplitude.

## Standing waves

When two identical waves travel through the same medium at the same time but in opposite directions, a special interference pattern called a standing wave is formed. Within a standing wave, regions of constructive interference are called antinodes and regions of destructive interference are called nodes. This name is derived from the impression that the wave appears to be 'standing still' since the nodes and antinodes are not being translated from one end of the medium to the other even though the wave's energy is continuously travelling 'back and forth'.

The lowest frequency to produce a standing wave pattern in a medium is called the fundamental or the 1st harmonic. As additional 'loops' are inserted, overtones are produced. A loop equals a distance of ½ $\lambda$. In each case, since the medium has not changed, the wave speed remains constant and we see evidence of the relationship that the wavelength is inversely proportional to the frequency.

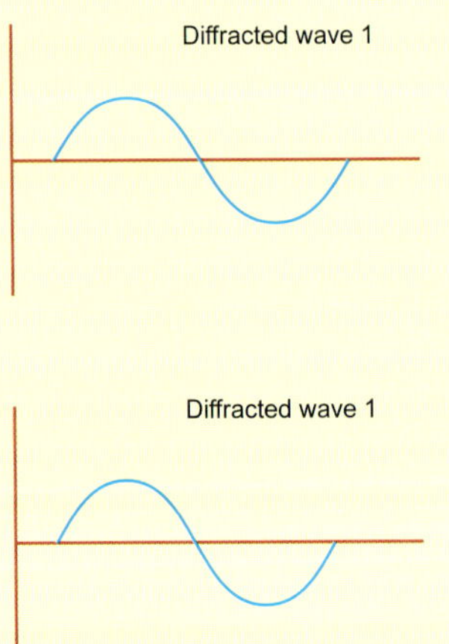


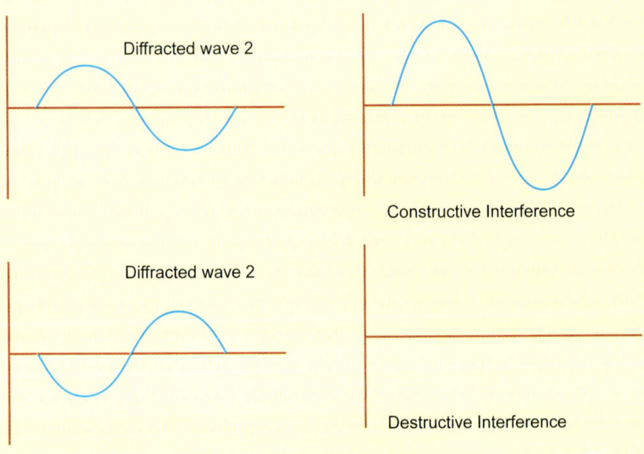

# Sound waves

Sound waves exist as variations of pressure in a medium such as air. They are created by the vibration of an object, which causes the air surrounding it to vibrate. The vibrating air then causes the human eardrum to vibrate, which the brain interprets as sound. Thus, a sound wave is a type of pressure wave caused by the vibration of an object in a conductive medium such as air. When the object vibrates, it sends out a series of waves which can be interpreted as sound. For example, when someone hits a drum, it causes the membrane of the drum to vibrate and the vibration is transmitted through the air, where it can reach the ear of a listener. Not all sound waves are in audible range. Humans hear around 20 Hz to 20 kHz, meaning that sounds above and below this range cannot usually be heard. Some animals can hear at higher and lower ranges.

Everyday our world is filled with a multitude of sounds. Sound is the main medium of communication. It lets us communicate with others or let others communicate with us. It can be a warning of danger or simply an enjoyable experience. The ability to hear is definitely an important sense, but people who are deaf are remarkable in the ways that they can compensate for their loss of hearing.

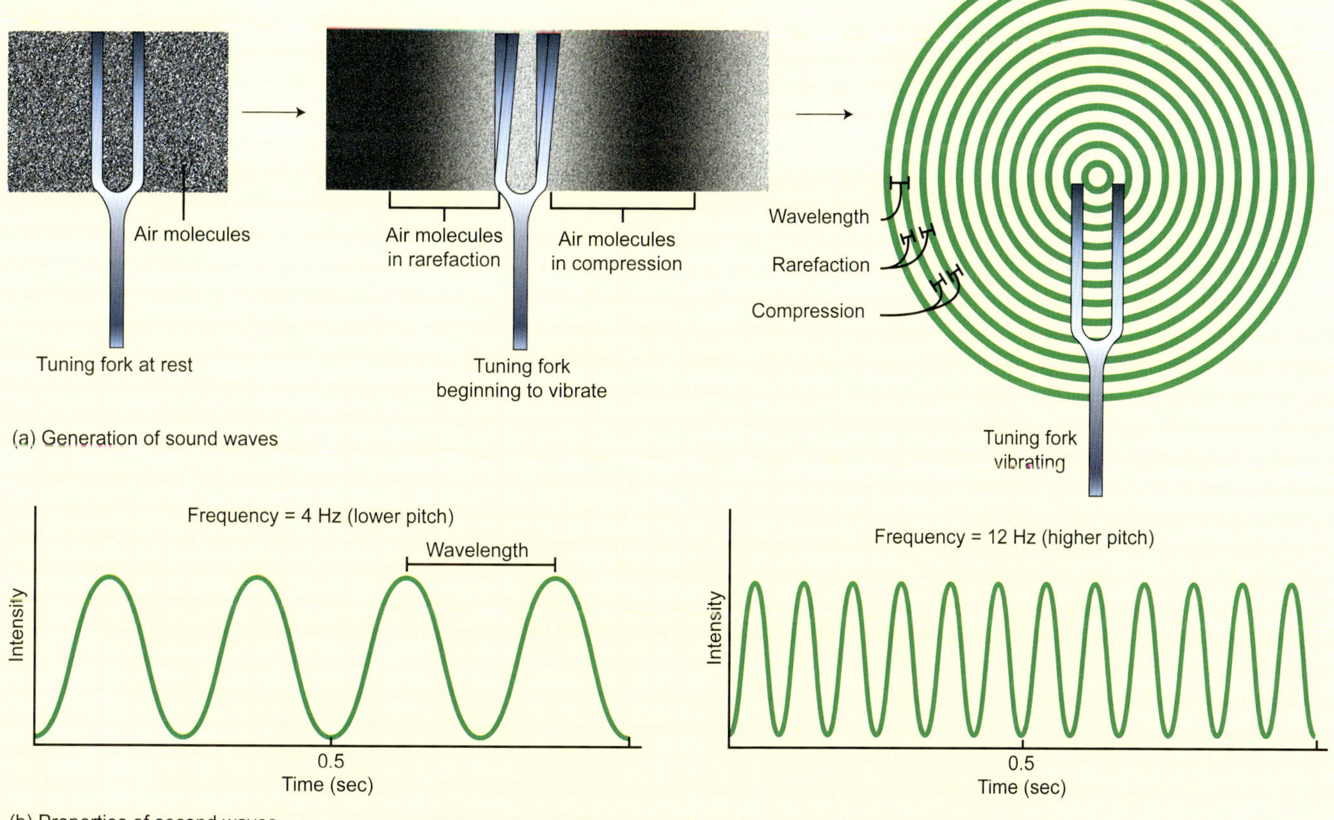


(a) Generation of sound waves

(b) Properties of second waves

# How does sound travel?

We hear the sounds because mechanical energy produced are transferred to our ears through the movement of atomic particles. Thus, sound is a pressure disturbance that moves through a medium in the form of mechanical waves. When a force is exerted on an atom, it moves from its rest or equilibrium position and exerts a force on the adjacent particles. These adjacent particles are moved from their rest position and this continues throughout the medium. This transfer of energy from one particle to the next is how sound travels through a medium.

Waves of sound energy move outward in all directions from the source. Without energy, there would be no sound. Sound waves are made up of compressions and rarefactions. Compression happens when particles are forced or pressed, together while rarefaction occurs when particles are given extra space and allowed to expand. Remember that sound is a type of kinetic energy. As the particles are moved from their rest position, they exert a force of the adjacent particles and pass the kinetic energy. Thus, sound energy travels outward from the source.

Sound travels through air, water or a block of steel. Thus, all of these are mediums of sound propagation. Without a medium there are no particles to carry the sound waves. A particle is tiny concentration of matter capable of transmitting energy. A particle could be an atom or a molecule. In places like space, where there is no atmosphere, there are only a few atomic particles to transfer the sound energy.

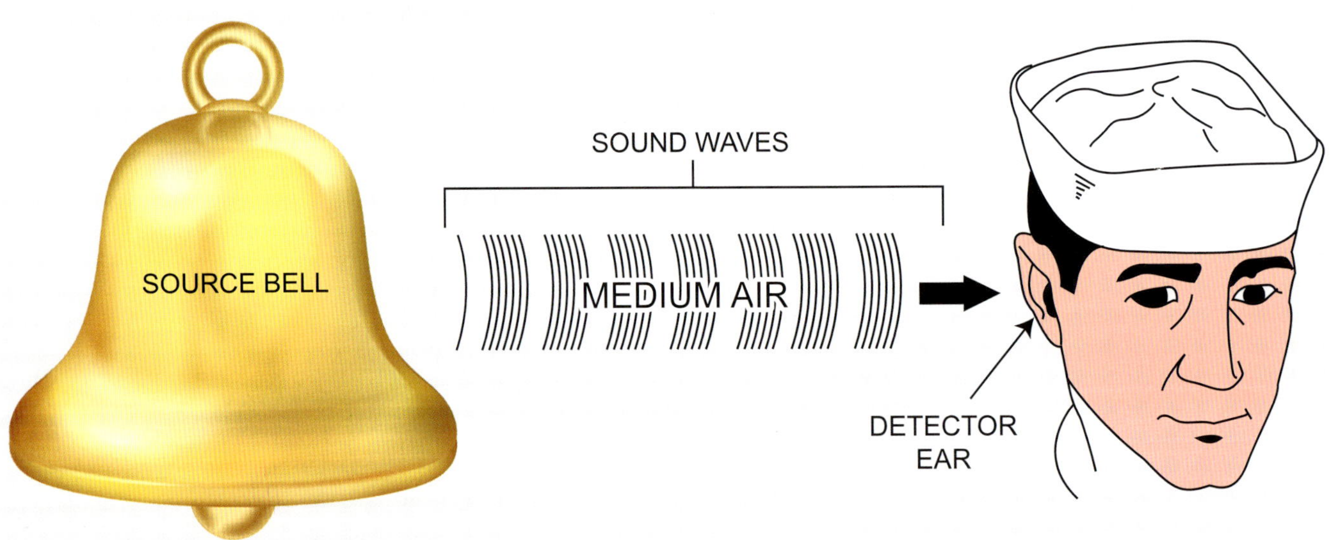

# Compression and rarefaction of sound waves

Sound is a form of energy propagated in the form of longitudinal waves. This energy causes the sensation of hearing on reaching the ear. Any vibrating body could be a source of sound. An excited tuning fork, the plucked wire of a stringed instrument, a bell struck with a hammer, a vibrating air column in a trumpet could be some of the examples. The sound produced by the source is propagated through a medium in the form of compressions and rarefactions.

We know that compression has a higher density than normal while rarefaction has lower density and together these two elements make up a sound wave. This sound is what we hear when something is hit or played. If you look at any normal visual representation of a sound wave, the humps above the middle line are called compression, the humps below, rarefaction.

Thus, compression and rarefaction are the segments of one cycle of a sound wave during its travel or motion. A succession of rarefactions and compressions makes up the sound wave motion that emanates from an acoustic source. Compression is the point when the most force is being applied to a molecule and rarefaction is the point when the least force is applied.

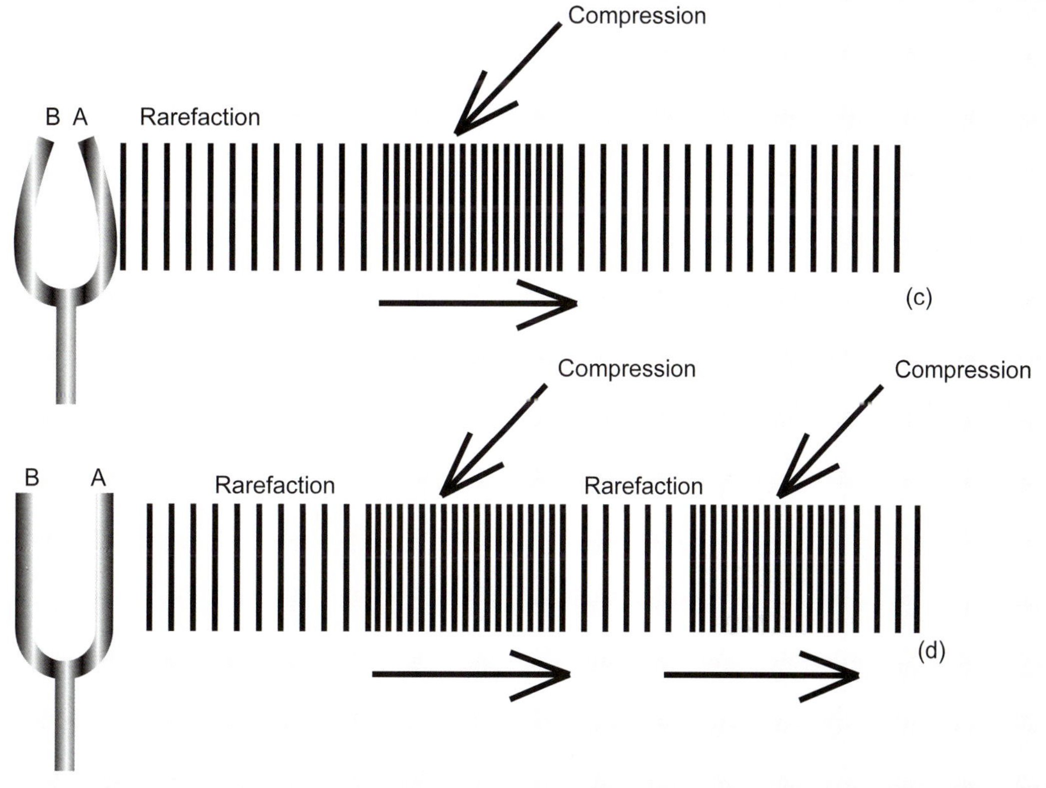

# Why are sounds different?

As you know, there are many different sounds. Fire alarms are loud, whispers are soft, and every one of your friends has a different voice. The differences between sounds are caused by intensity, pitch and tone.

## Intensity

Sound is a wave and waves have amplitude or height. Amplitude is a measure of energy. The more energy a wave has, the higher its amplitude. As amplitude increases, intensity also increases. Intensity is the amount of energy a sound has over an area. The same sound is more intense if you hear it in a smaller area. In general, we call sounds with a higher intensity louder. We are used to measuring the sounds we hear in loudness. The sound of your friend yelling is loud, while the sound of your own breathing is very soft. Loudness cannot be assigned a specific number, but intensity can. Intensity is measured in decibels. The human ear is more sensitive to high sounds, so they may seem louder than a low noise of the same intensity. Decibels and intensity, however, do not depend on the ear. They can be measured with instruments. A whisper is about 10 decibels while thunder is 100 decibels. Listening to loud sounds, sounds with intensities above 85 decibels, may damage your ears. If a noise is loud enough, over 120 decibels, it can be painful to listen to. One hundred and twenty decibels is the threshold of pain.

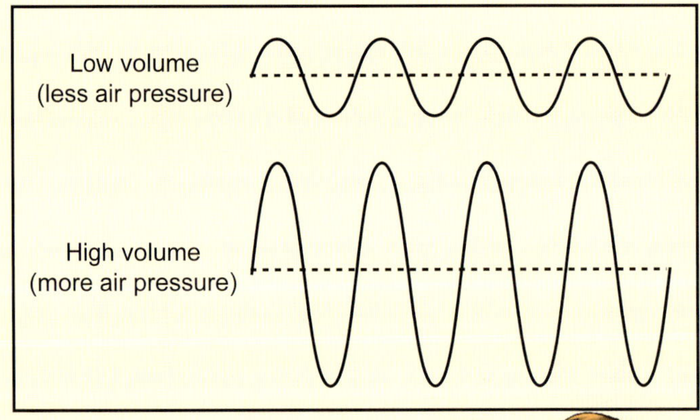


## Do it yourself

**Sound differences:** Pitch is the highness or lowness of a sound. Hold the edge of a card against a bicycle wheel. Revolve the wheel slowly and then gradually faster and faster. The faster you spin the bicycle wheel, the higher the sound will become.

**Explanation:** Pitch depends on the number of vibrations per second. The more are vibrations, the higher is the pitch.

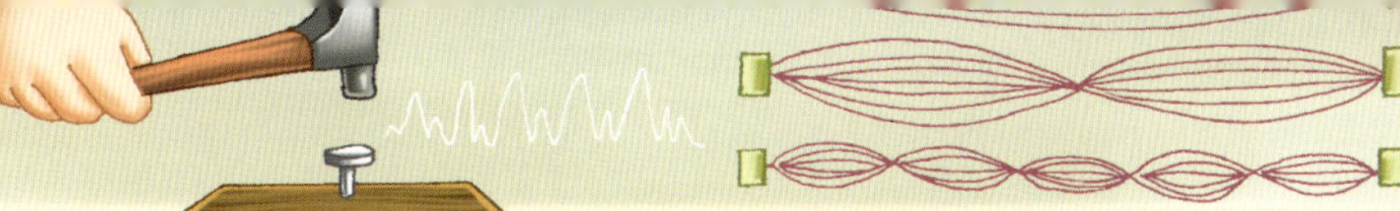

## Pitch

Pitch helps us distinguish between low and high sounds. Imagine that a singer sings the same note twice, one an octave above the other. You can hear a difference between these two sounds. That is because their pitch is different. Pitch depends on the frequency of a sound wave. Frequency, in turn, is the number of wavelengths that fit into one unit of time. So, even though the singer sang the same note twice, we heard them as different because the sounds had different frequencies. Frequencies are measured in hertz. One hertz is equal to one cycle of compression and rarefaction per second. High sounds have high frequencies and low sounds have low frequencies. Thunder has a frequency of only 50 hertz, while a whistle can have a frequency of 1,000 hertz.

The human ear is able to hear frequencies of 20 to 20,000 hertz. Some animals can hear sounds at even higher frequencies.

The reason we cannot hear dog whistles, while they can, is because the frequency of the whistle is too high to be processed by our ears. Sounds that are too high for us to hear are called ultrasonic.

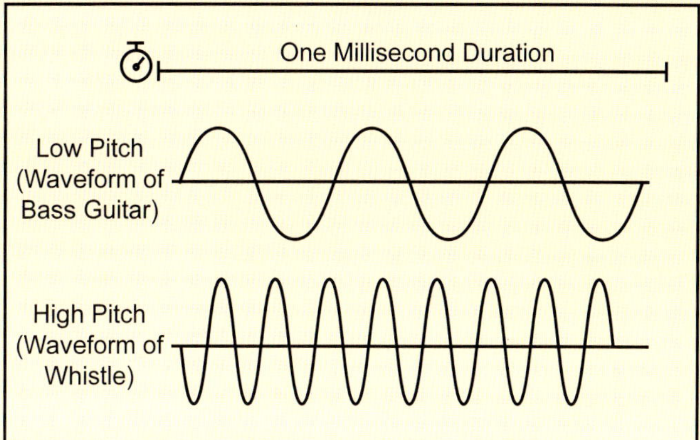


Ultrasonic waves have many uses. In nature, bats emit ultrasonic waves and listen to the echoes to help them know where walls are or to find prey. Captains of submarines and other boats use special machines that send out and receive ultrasonic waves. These waves help them guide their boats through the water and warn them when another boat is near.

## Do it yourself

**Blowing sounds:** Press the top edge of an empty bottle to your lower lip and blow lightly across the top. Pour in a little water and blow again. Then add more water and blow. You will see that more water you add, higher sound will be.

**Explanation:** You are vibrating the air in the bottle. When you add water you leave less room for air. The less air there is in the bottle, faster it vibrates and higher the sound. In the same way, higher notes on a musical instrument are made by shortening the air column.

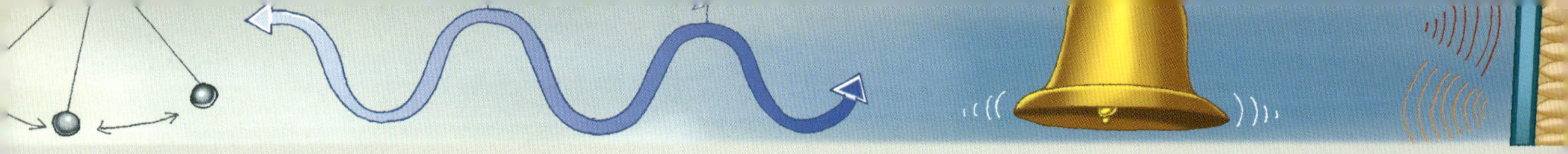

## Tone and harmonics

Another difference you may have noticed between sounds is that some sounds are pleasant while others are unpleasant. A beginner violin player sounds very different than a violin player in a symphony, even if they are playing the same note. A violin also sounds different than a flute playing the same pitch. This is because they have a different tone or sound quality. When a source vibrates, it actually vibrates with many frequencies at the same time. Each of those frequencies produces a wave. Sound quality depends on the combination of different frequencies of sound waves. Imagine a guitar string tightly stretched. If we strum it, the energy from our finger is transferred to the string, causing it to vibrate. When the whole string vibrates, we hear the lowest pitch. This pitch is called the fundamental. Remember, the fundamental is really only one of many pitches that the string is producing. Parts of the string vibrating at frequencies higher than the fundamental are called overtones, while those vibrating in whole number multiples of the fundamental are called harmonics. A frequency of two times the fundamental will sound one octave higher and is called the second harmonic. A frequency four times the fundamental will sound two octaves higher and is called the fourth harmonic. Because the fundamental is one times itself, it is also called the first harmonic.

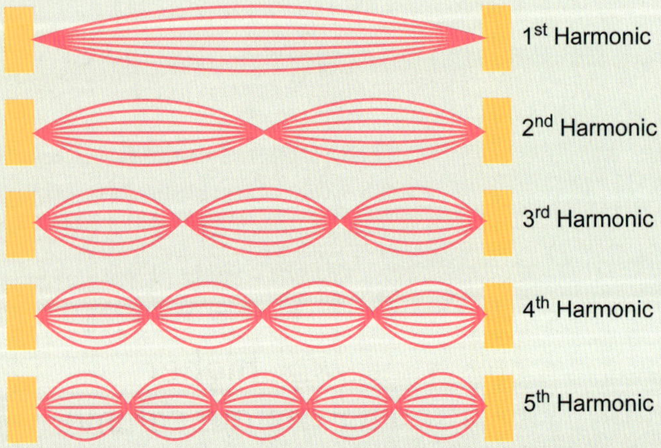

1st Harmonic

2nd Harmonic

3rd Harmonic

4th Harmonic

5th Harmonic

## What is the difference between music and noise?

Some sounds, like construction work, falling objects, cracking sounds, traffic horns are unpleasant. While others, such as music, are enjoyable to listen. If this is the only way to tell the difference between noise and music, everyone's opinion will be different. The sound of rain might be pleasant music to you, while the sound of your little brother practicing piano might be an unpleasant noise! To help classify sounds, there are three properties which a sound must have to be musical. A sound must have an identifiable pitch, a good or pleasing quality of tone, and repeating pattern or rhythm to be music. Noise on the other hand has no identifiable pitch, no pleasing tone and no steady rhythm.

## Sound wave interference

When two or more sound waves from different sources are present at the same time, they interact with each other to

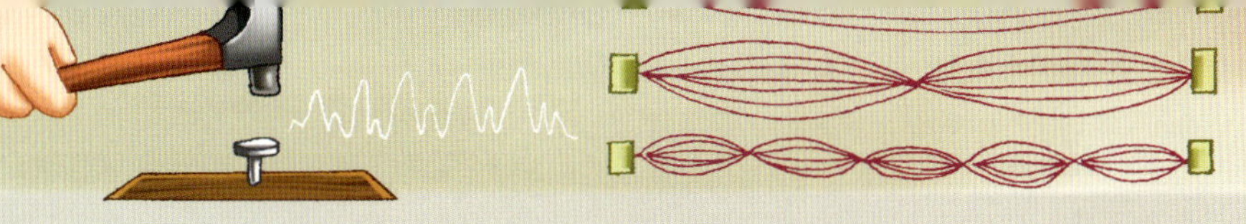



produce a new wave. The new wave is the sum of all the different waves. Wave interaction is called **interference**. If the compressions and the rarefactions of the two waves line up, they strengthen each other and create a wave with a higher intensity. This type of interference is known as constructive.

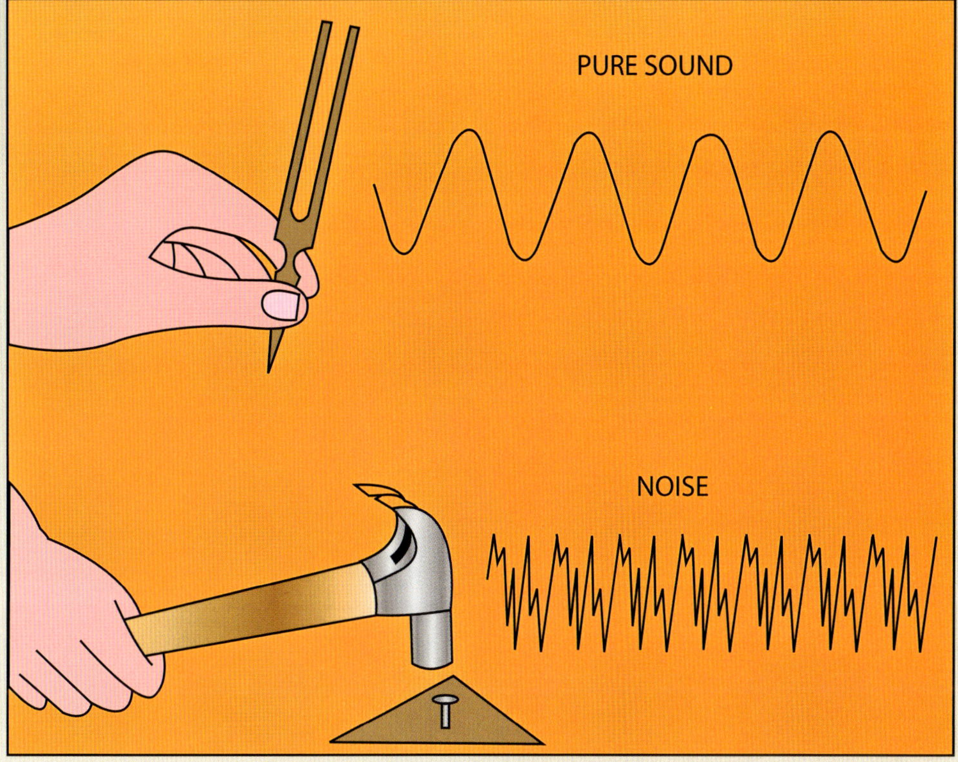


When the compressions and rarefactions are out of phase, their interaction creates a wave with a dampened or lower intensity. This is destructive interference. When waves are interfering with each other destructively, the sound is louder in some places and softer in others. As a result, we hear pulses or beats in the sound.

**Famous Mathematician Pythagoras, in 6th century B.C., observed a musician plucking a stringed instrument and noticed that the amplitude of a vibration was related to the perceived loudness of the sound. He also noticed that sound stopped when the vibrations were stopped and shorter strings vibrated more rapidly, producing high-pitch sound.**

**Dogs can hear higher frequency sounds than humans, allowing them to hear some noises that we can not. Some animals use sounds to detect danger which alert them about a possible attack before it happens.**

# Sound travelling through materials

It is a known fact that sounds travel faster in some materials than others. Sound waves travel outward in straight lines from their source until something interferes with their path. When sound changes mediums, or enters a different material, it is bent from its original direction. This change in angle of direction is called **refraction**. Refraction is caused by sound entering the new medium at an angle. Because of the angle, part of the wave enters the new medium first and changes speed. The difference in speeds causes the wave to bend.

The angle of refraction depends on the angle that the waves has when it enters the new medium. As the angle from the wave to the barrier between the two mediums gets smaller, the angle of refraction also gets closer to the barrier. When the wave's entering angle reaches a certain point, called the critical angle, the refraction is parallel to the dividing line between the mediums. The critical angle depends on the two mediums the sound is coming from and going to. The speed of sound is different in every medium. Because of this, even if the sound hits at the same angle, the angle of refraction will vary for different mediums. The greater the difference in speed between the two mediums, the greater the critical angle will be.

## Do it yourself

**Sound travels better through wood or solid objects than air or water:** Blow into a re-sealable bag or a balloon and then seal it. Place the inflated bag next to your ear and gently tap it with the eraser part of the pencil. Now, fill the bag with water - half filled - and seal it. Repeat the experiment by tapping on the bag with the pencil. Compare both of the sounds. Finally, instead of using the bag, Use a wooden block instead of bag, keep it near your ear and tap the block with the pencil. Does it sound much different than previous sounds?

Explanation: Sound waves travel easier through solid objects and sound better.

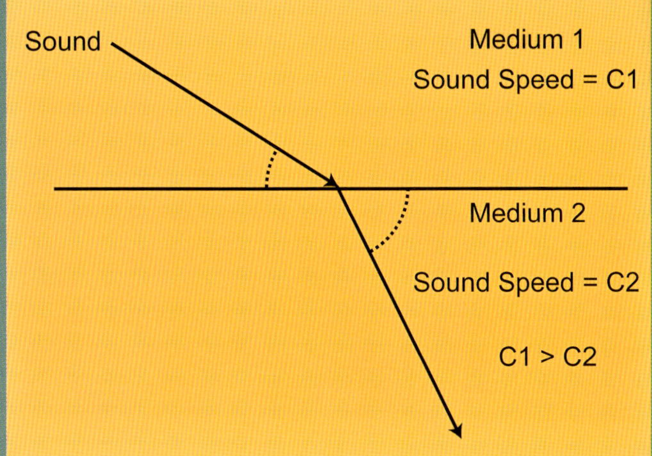


If sound hits the new medium with any angle smaller than the critical angle, it will not be able to enter. Instead it will bounce off, or be reflected, from the dividing line. When a wave is reflected, it returns with an angle equal to the one with which it hit. Whenever sound hits a new medium, part of it is reflected back. The rest enters the new medium and is refracted. Imagine that sound is travelling through the air and hits the wall of a brick building. Some of the wave is reflected, but much of it enters the brick. The part of the wave going through the brick is now going faster than the part in the air. This is because brick is a solid whose molecules are closer together and can transmit sound more quickly. This difference in speeds caused the wave to bend or be refracted.

Suppose that the wave hits the building with an angle that is smaller than its critical angle. This time, the wave cannot enter the brick and all of it is reflected. If the wave struck the wall with an angle of 15 degrees, it would reflect back with the same angle from the other side. Since there are 180 degrees total, the reflected angle would be 165 degrees, 15 degrees measured from the other direction.

## Do it yourself

**Hearing with spoons:** Demonstrate how your ears hear with this activity. Cut a piece of string about 2 ft. long. Attach a metal spoon to the middle of the string using a rubber band. Wrap the ends of the string around the index finger on each hand. Rest the tips of your index fingers in your ears. Stand next to a counter, table or chair and sway slightly until the spoon bangs against the surface. When the spoon hits the surface it causes the string to vibrate; these vibrations travel up the string and to your ears, causing your eardrums to vibrate. Your brain translates these vibrations into sound.

# Reflection of sound

When sound is incident on a solid or a liquid surface it bounces off the surface like light rays. Sound waves also obey the laws of reflection. For sound waves to reflect, we need extended surface or obstacle of large size. For example, the rolling of thunder is due to successive reflections from clouds and land surfaces. When sound reflects off a special curved surface called a parabola, it will bounce out in a straight line no matter where it originally hits. Many stages are designed as parabolas so the sound will go directly into the audience, instead of bouncing around on stage. If the parabola is closed off by another curved surface, it is called an ellipse. Sound will travel from one focus to the other, no matter where it strikes the wall. For example, a whispering gallery is designed as an ellipse. If your friend stands at one focus and you stand at the other, his whisper will be heard clearly by you. No one in the rest of the room will hear anything.

Reflection is responsible for many interesting wave phenomena. Echoes are the sound of our own voice reflecting back to our ears. The sound we hear ringing in an auditorium after the sound has been stopped playing is caused by reflection off the walls and other objects. A sound wave will continue to bounce around a room, until it has lost all its energy. A wave has some of its energy absorbed by the objects it hits. The rest is lost as heat energy.

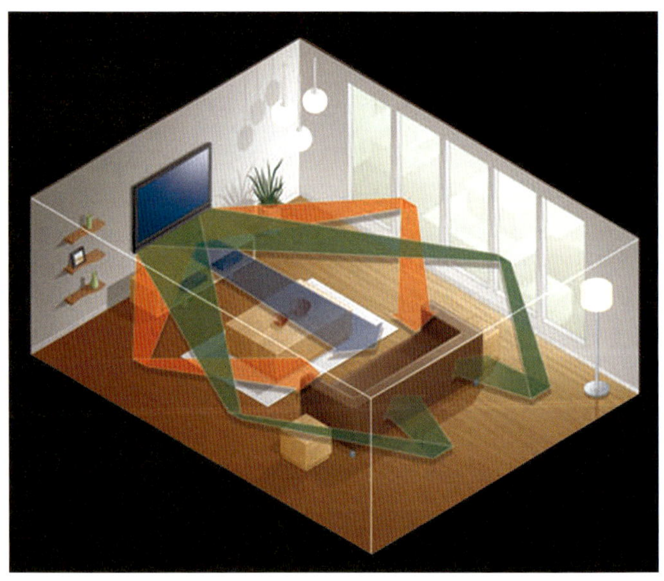

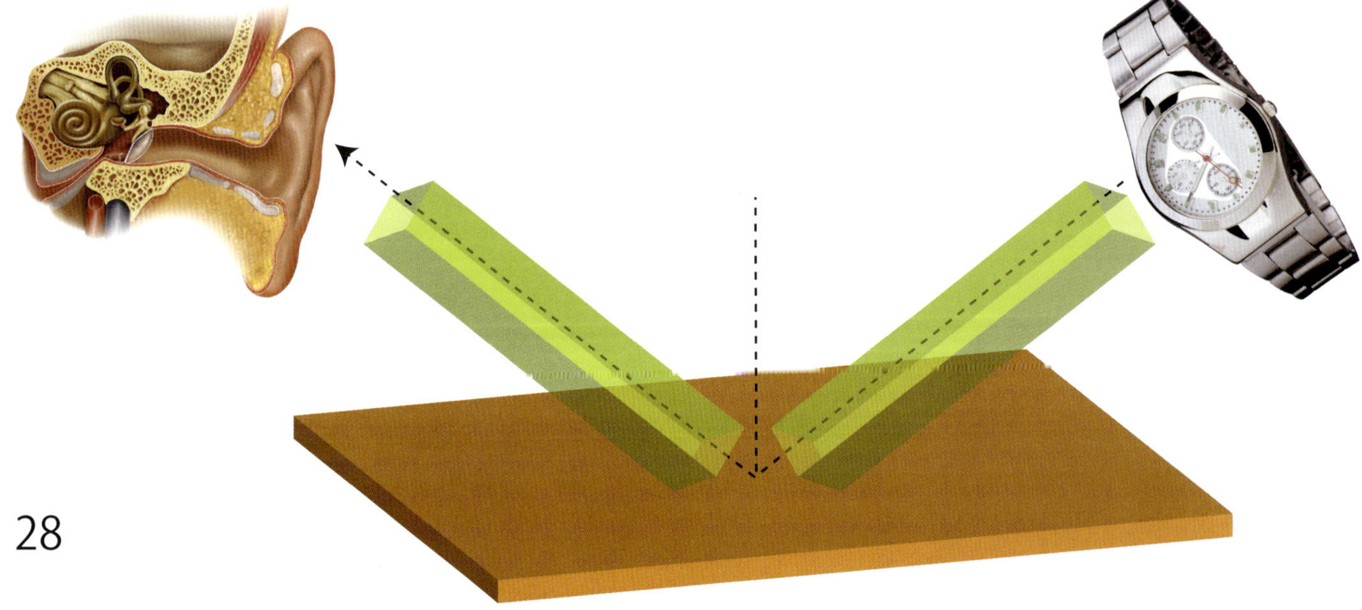

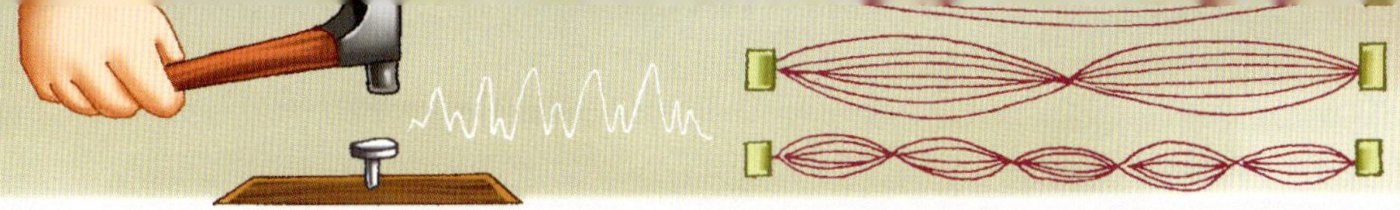



# Sound absorption

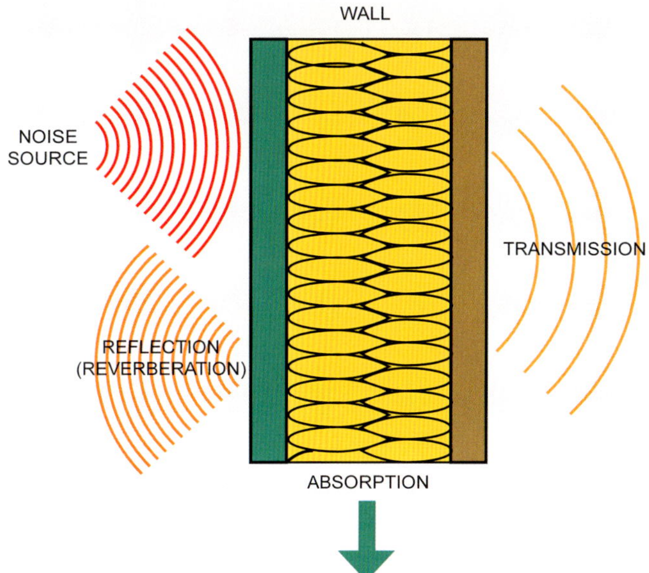


Everything, even air, absorbs sound. The process, by which the intensity of sound is diminished by the conversion of the energy of the sound wave into heat, is called sound absorption. The absorption of sound is an important case of sound attenuation. Regardless of the material through which sound passes, its intensity is measured by the average flow of energy. It is the wave per unit time per unit area perpendicular to the direction of propagation. It decreases with distance from the source. This decrease is called attenuation. In the simple case of a point source of sound radiating into an ideal medium, the intensity decreases inversely as the square of the distance from the source. This relationship exists because the spherical area through which the energy propagates per unit time increases as the square of the propagation distance.

Sound absorption in fluids can be measured in a variety of ways, referred to as mechanical, optical, electrical, and thermal methods. All these methods reduce essentially to a measurement of sound intensity as a function of distance from the source. The amount of sound that air absorbs increases with audio frequency and decreases with air density, but also depends on temperature and humidity. Sound absorption in air depends heavily on relative humidity. Sound absorption in water is generally much less than in air. It also rises with frequency, and it strongly depends on the amount of dissolved materials. Sound absorbing materials are used in construction of sound proof rooms.

# Sound absorption coefficient

The sound absorption coefficient indicates how much of the sound is absorbed in the actual material. The absorption coefficient varies with the frequency of sound.

The absorption coefficient can be expressed as:

$$\alpha = I_a / I_i$$

Where, $I_a$ = sound intensity absorbed (W/m2 )

$I_i$ = incident sound intensity (W/m2)

## How does sound reach every point in the room?

Though sound travels in a straight path from its source, still it gets around corners.

You already know that if you and your friend are standing on either side of a wall and there is an open door nearby, you will be able to hear what your friend says. You hear your friend because of sound diffraction. Diffraction uses the edges of a barrier as a secondary sound source that sends waves in a new direction. These secondary waves overlap and interfere with each other and the original waves, making the sound less clear. Working together, diffraction and reflection can send sounds to every part of a room.

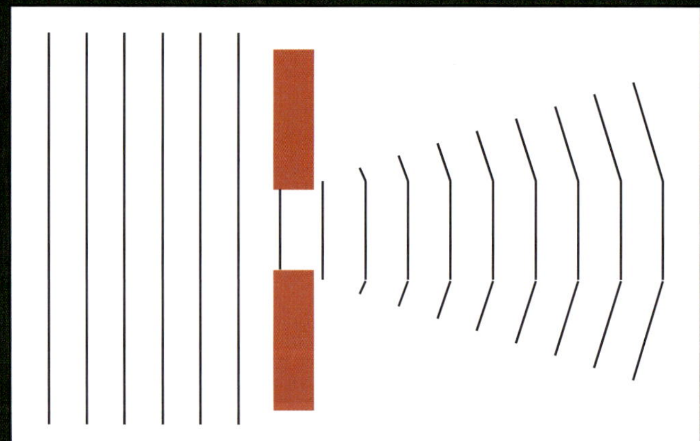

# Test Your MEMORY

1. What is a wave?
2. Explain the vibratory motion of a simple pendulum.
3. What is the difference between transverse and longitudinal waves?
4. Describe the simple harmonic motion.
5. Define surface waves.
6. Explain the interference of waves.
7. What is the relation between frequency and time-period of a wave?
8. Write down the wave equation.
9. What are the sound waves?
10. What is the difference between compression and rarefaction?
11. How does sound travel from one medium to other?
12. What is the difference between music and noise?

# Index